TRAMWAYS IN BRITAIN ON OLD PICTURE POSTCARDS

Norman Ellis

1. A trial run for tram no. 10 of the Hastings Tramways Co. on 15th July 1905, sixteen days before the official opening.

£3.95

'A long ride on a modern tramcar may not lay claim to the romantic associations of travel in the old coaching days, nor the wild adventure of knight-errantry, but it is a jolly sight more expeditious and comfortable; and with a little imagination it may be invested with something of the spirit of mild adventure. Even when the way runs through the town, there is much to engross the attention of the student of men and urban affairs, and vistas are opened out, which, though commonplace in themselves, are absolutely picturesque when seen under certain phases and varying atmospheric conditions' - The Bradford Picturesque Tram Guide published circ. 1903 by H.M. Trotter and Co., Albion Court, Bradford.

**Designed and Published by
Reflections of a Bygone Age,
Keyworth, Nottingham.
1986**

**Printed by
Adlard Print and Typesetting Services,
Ruddington, Notts.**

ISBN 0 946245 13 4

THE AUTHOR

Following interest aroused by reading books on tramways, Norman Ellis began collecting old postcards of trams in 1967. Eventually his collection was considerably pruned to comprise mainly real-photographic cards. Norman now collects other good photographic social history postcards, particularly any which show activity or are connected with transport. Books and ephemera also feature prominently in his collection. Photography is another interest. Norman lived for many years at Outwood, near Wakefield, but now resides at Ossett, Yorkshire, and is employed as a senior draughtsman with a local engineering company.

All illustrations in this book are from postcards in the author's collection. All coloured originals are reproduced in colour. Most other illustrations are from real-photographic type cards. Where they are not, this is stated (if not otherwise obvious).

TRAM POSTCARDS

Variety

Two features which distinguished British tramways from those in many other parts of the civilised world were the lack of integrated inter-urban systems and the preponderance and variety of double-deck cars. The first and, to some extent the second, contributed to the demise rather than the development of tramways, with the result that trams in the British Isles have become little more than a part of history. But let nobody deny the important part which they played in the lives of people, particularly during the first three decades of the twentieth century. Some of the very characteristics which caused their downfall have helped to contribute to the rich array of old tram postcards, which provide a source of interest for tramway historian and postcard collector.

Printed Cards

These are usually based on photographs and may be black and white, sepia or coloured. The better black and white or sepia cards can be almost as good as real-photographic ones, a good example being those produced by Louis Levy. Coloured cards can be far removed from the original views. Colours, either applied by hand or intrinsic with the printing, may be incorrect. Some coloured cards were derived from paintings, for example Tuck Oilettes.

Real-photographic Cards

These may be black and white or sepia. Some were produced by the larger companies; good examples are those done by W.H. Smith and Son or, on a more local basis, E.L. Scrivens. The rarer cards were usually produced by a small company or an individual photographer. These may have mis-spelt captions, superficial fingerprints and some fading, but any shortcomings are often amply compensated by the rarity of the view and the atmosphere it evokes.

Value

Within the above two divisions, numerous tram card types exist, from the common coloured street scene with a distant tram to the superbly clear photographic close-up tram, the latter perhaps being worth over one hundred times more than the former. Many factors, including condition, govern the price of a card but possibly the chief criterion is the adage of supply and demand. Some collectors prefer postally used cards, to others this is immaterial.

977 LONDON. — Westminster Bridge. — LL.

2. This printed postcard of Westminster Bridge, London, was no. 277 in the LL (Louis Levy) series. It was well-produced and, because it showed a famous landmark (Houses of Parliament with Big Ben) and one of the renowned London trams, probably would be a popular seller, both as a souvenir and for posting home. This helps to explain why, nowadays, it turns up fairly regularly. Although the view is on a bridge, the card really ranks as a street scene.

Street Scenes

A large number of tram postcards belong to this category. Cards can appear in any of the printed or photographic types. The tram may be distant or prominent; it may be there by accident or the photographer may have waited for it to appear. This section includes common and rare views. Generally, town backstreets or suburbs are more desirable than city centres.

Seaside Views

Most of these are really street scenes. Promenade views, usually of the printed type, often coloured, were intended for mass sale to extol the virtues of the resort. Any trams featured are usually middle-distant. The scarcer cards are of locations away from the sea-front; these are often real-photographic.

Termini

This is basically a sub-division of the street scene but deserves special mention. Mostly, the cards are real-photographic and quite rare. The tram terminus seemed to be a recognised location. The tram is often middle-distant or prominent but occasionally non-existent. This latter type can be of interest if there is track or wiring layout. The car may be in sharper focus because the photographer would be able to capture it whilst stationary.

Track Laying

These rare cards are usually real-photographic and often full of action.

Tramway Openings

These were events not to be missed, and the local photographer would find a ready sale for souvenir postcards. Usually cards are real-photographic, but printed versions were produced, even some in colour. The tram is usually in close-up, perhaps laden with civic dignitaries and surrounded by an enthusiastic crowd. Some exceptionally good cards exist in this category.

Decorated Cars

There are two main types — trams decorated for a special occasion such as a royal visit and trams decorated for an advertising campaign such as an army recruitment or a shopping week. Cards may be real-photographic or printed, including coloured. Some coloured cards are quite garish. The tram, whether captured at the depot or on a street, usually occupies most of the view. There seems less enthusiasm for collecting this type of card, possibly because the fairy lights and bunting obscure the tram.

Accidents

These are predominantly real-photographic, but some printed versions exist. The frequency of appearance of these cards is not an indication that tram disasters were an everyday happening; rather that the local photographer had an eye for making money. With a little enterprise, the cards could be on sale in local shops on the day following or within a few days of the disaster. Some accidents appear on only one or two different cards; other accidents have numerous different cards with the disaster viewed from all angles.

Architecture

Compared with railway architecture, most tramway architectural features were ordinary. Tramsheds or depots tended to be austere buildings, functional rather than fancy. Interiors or exteriors of these structures may be found, usually on real-photographic cards; tram or trams are usually visible. Street scenes, particularly photographic types are worth examination for features such as passenger shelters, stop signs and overhead wire standards, the last of which could be very ornate.

597 Soho Rd. & C... ...dsworth Birmingham

3. Compared with the previous London postcard, this real-photographic view of Soho Road and the Council House at Handsworth, a suburb of Birmingham, would have a narrower sales appeal and therefore be produced in smaller quantities. It is, though, a superb example of a local postcard producer's skill. Every detail is sharply defined on the original card. Shops, pork butcher's wagon, tram standards, tram stop, tram with people boarding - all these invite closer scrutiny. A type of card now much sought-after by local collectors and, although the nearest tram is only middle-distant, a 'must' for the tram card collector. A street scene par excellence.

Staff

The people who kept the trams operational sometimes feature on real-photographic cards. It may be a portrait of the driver and/or conductor in their uniforms, a group of wartime clippies, or the maintenance men in their overalls in the depot yard. It could even be the tramway brass band or cricket team.

Close-ups

Cards exist, usually real-photographic and often superb, where the tram occupies a substantial part of the view, but which do not slot into any of the above categories. The car may have driver and conductor posed in front. Some of these photographs were probably taken to show these gentlemen; it is fortunate that, in many cases, the whole tram is visible. If the view is not captioned, its location may be identifiable from the destination display, coat-of-arms or company crest, design of vehicle or its background.

Comic Cards

These are invariably printed type, usually in colour. They find a place in some tram card collections. Commonest seem to be the coloured cards which show a heavily loaded car and a caption like 'Last tram to ....', where the name of a town was overprinted in the space provided, for sale in the particular locality.

Modern Cards/Reproductions

Although not strictly within the scope of this book, these are worth a mention (and a warning). There are various printed, including coloured, and photographic cards, some with plain backs. An interesting collection can be built up for a modest sum. But beware of photographs, usually produced from the forties onwards, often from much older and still-existing negatives, which masquerade as older items and are priced as such. Experienced collectors can usually spot them; new collectors should be careful.

ACKNOWLEDGMENTS

The following provided valuable assistance:-

Roy Brook of Huddersfield, a recognised tramway expert, who checked the introduction and captions, made necessary alterations and supplied additional information.
Brian Boyce of Hull.
Pat and Rennie Pickles of Wakefield.

BIBLIOGRAPHY

The following books etc. were particularly useful:-

Great British Tramway Networks by Wingate H. Bett and John C. Gillham (Light Railway Transport League)
The Golden Age of Tramways by Charles Klapper (Routledge and Kegan Paul)
Tramway Heyday by J. Joyce (Ian Allan)
The British Tram by Frank E. Wilson (Percival Marshall)
The Tramways of Northumberland by George S. Hearse (G.S. Hearse)
The London Tramcar 1861-1952 by R.W. Kidner (Oakwood Press)
Tramways of the West of England by P.W. Gentry (Light Railway Transport League)
North Wales Tramways by Keith Turner (David and Charles)

Various regional booklets adapted from **Great British Tramway Networks** by J.H. Price (Light Rail Transit Association, formerly Light Railway Transport League)

Various monthly issues of **Modern Tramway** (Ian Allan/Light Rail Transit Association)

Various quarterly issues of **Tramway Review** (Light Rail Transit Association)

TRAMWAY HISTORY

Social changes

The nineteenth and twentieth centuries brought great social changes in the British Isles, not least in the field of transport. The horse had long been regarded as the motive power for most forms of conveyance. In the nineteenth century, buses and trams, canals, even early railways, used horses. Eventually the horse was largely superseded by steam and electric traction and the internal combustion engine. That great phenomenon, the steam railway, came and went in little over a hundred years. The electric tram did not last as long. This is the age of the private car, the one-man bus, motorways, juggernauts, inter-city rail and fast air travel. Here is a book about the past. There is now a revival of interest in earlier forms of transport.

Beginnings

The year when trams were first operated in the British Isles is debatable, not because the facts are unknown, but because of similarities between early railways and tramways. Subsequently, perhaps the best distinction was that a tramway ran along a street, a railway did not, but there were exceptions to defy the rule. It is generally reckoned that fare-paying passengers were first carried by rail in 1807 from Swansea to Oystermouth. This line was the forerunner of both the passenger-carrying railway and tramway. In 1859, trams were carrying people on the tracks normally used for freight in the streets of Liverpool's dock area. Prior to this, there had been street railroads in New York and other American cities. From America came George Francis Train who, in 1860, succeeded in starting a 1¼ mile long passenger tramway at Birkenhead. In 1861, Train opened three street tramways in London and one in Darlington. The ventures in London had disappeared by 1862; the Darlington line lasted two years. Failure was partly due to the step rail which protruded above the road and angered other road users. G.F. Train opened a line in the Potteries in 1862. This was saved from extinction because the step rail was replaced by a grooved rail laid flush with the roadway, which became standard practice in later years. A frustrated G.F. Train left England in 1862 after his efforts to start tramways in towns such as Glasgow, Manchester, Newcastle and Portsmouth had failed. But trams did appear in Portsmouth in 1865.

Tramways Act

An important step in British tramway history was the passing of the Tramways Act of 1870. Although intended to facilitate construction and regulate the working of tramways, some clauses cast harmful obstacles. The act stated that tramway operators were responsible for maintenance of the roadway between the lines and for 18in. on either side. The compilers of the act had in mind the damage which horses hooves might cause. Another crippling effect of the act was that a local authority could compulsorily purchase the tramway undertaking after 21 years and at 7-year intervals thereafter. This fear of being taken over deterred many operators from spending large sums of money on developing their tram systems.

Horse Trams

By 1876, there were 136 miles of tram track in the British Isles. All tramcars were pulled by horses. Some were single-deck cars seating approximately sixteen passengers, pulled by a single horse. Many were open-top double-deck cars which seated over forty people and required a pair of horses. On a steep hill, an additional horse, or horses, might be added. The largest double-deck bus, pulled by two horses, would seat, at most, 25 passengers. The smooth tram tracks, as opposed to the rough roads, facilitated the use of trams which were substantially larger than contemporary buses.

Steam Trams

It was a logical step that the great invention of the Victorian age, the steam locomotive, should be applied to the street tramway. Govan, near Glasgow, was the first to have a regular steam tram service through its streets in 1877, although earlier experiments had occurred in other places. The Tramways Act of 1879 authorised the operation of trams by mechanical power, but this did not mean that no more horse cars were placed in service. Unlike the horse tram, the steam tram was confined to particular areas, notably the North and Midlands. A steam tram consisted of the tram engine and passenger trailer. The tram engine, which burned coke, worked on a similar principle to the railway locomotive, but looked different. The Board of Trade stipulated that the machinery should be concealed and noise kept to a minimum, therefore the engine was encased in a box-like structure. Due to increased power, the passenger car could be larger than the horse equivalent. A typical vehicle would be double-decked and seat sixty passengers. Some cars, particularly in early days, had open upper-decks, but the top-cover found favour because it offered protection from soot and sparks. Eventually over 500 steam trams were operating in the British Isles.

Electric Breakthrough

The clip-clop of the horse's hooves and the puffing and hissing of the steam engine were not to last for ever. Experiments in electrical propulsion were taking place. In 1883, Magnus Volk opened his electric tramway along the sea-front at Brighton, using the running rails for current pickup and return. Later the same year, a line from Portrush to Bushmills in Ulster used a third rail for current collection. Obviously these methods were unsuitable for streets. A major development came in 1885 when the first electric street tramway in the British Isles began operation at Blackpool. Current was taken from a conduit between the rails. The system had a measure of success but sand and sea-water entered the slot and caused short circuits. A significant breakthrough occurred in 1891. The system which was to become standard practice on most British tramways was introduced from Sheepscar to Roundhay on the outskirts of Leeds. Current was collected from overhead wires. These and the standards which supported them were aesthetically displeasing to many people. The method was clean, safe and functional

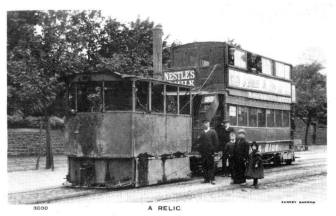

4. Simply titled 'A Relic', this card shows a steam tram engine and passenger trailer of the Barrow-in-Furness Tramway Co. Ltd. Steam trams operated in Barrow from 1885 to 1903. The view probably originated from the latter days because of the decrepit condition of the engine and the sag of the trailer. The card was no. 3000 in the series by Sankey of Barrow, a prolific postcard producer of the area.

5. The London County Council operated the largest tramway system in the British Isles. It evolved from various horse tramways which were taken over and electrified. With surrounding company and municipal systems, the complete network was huge and complex. In 1933, all came under the wing of the London Passenger Transport Board. This 1907 scene was captioned *'First Cars to Lee Green'*. It shows London County Council 'E' class bogie tram no. 497, built by Hurst Nelson and Co. Ltd. of Motherwell in 1907, and working by conduit collection. The view is made more attractive by its background and the enthusiastic crowd. Postmarked at Lee Sorting Office, 27th April 1907.

and gradually gained acceptance. By the end of the century, electric trams which worked from overhead wires were running in several British towns. In the last decade of the nineteenth century, many local authorities exercised their powers of compulsory purchase and bought out the local tramway company. The early part of the twentieth century saw tremendous tramway activity. By 1914, there were nearly 13,000 trams, altogether using 2500 miles of track. A serious contender was the petrol omnibus.

6. The smallest urban electric tramway system in the British Isles was at Taunton. It opened in 1901 and belonged to the Taunton and West Somerset Electric Railways and Tramways Co. Ltd. When ambitious plans did not materialise, the title was changed to the Taunton Electric Traction Co. Ltd. Of 3ft.6in. gauge, the one route was barely a mile long and, even with an extension in 1909, was still less than 1¾ miles. No. 4 of the original total fleet of six double-deck trams is shown here. When the track was re-laid in 1905, these trams were sold and replaced by six new single-deckers. The tramway closed in 1921. Posted from Taunton, 8th July 1907.

Electric Trams

Most electric trams took current from overhead wires. In a few areas, notably parts of London, it was taken from a conduit in the road. A further method not much favoured, was the surface contact system where a skate suspended below the tram picked up current from studs situated between the rails. Track gauges varied, the most common being 3ft. 6in., 4ft. and 4ft. 8½in., but there were others. Electric trams were of either single-truck or double-bogie type, thus running on four or eight wheels respectively. Single-deck cars usually had a roof. An unusual type of single-decker normally used on lines in holiday areas had no covering whatsoever, the seats extending the full width of the car; these were known as toastracks. Double-deck cars were sometimes open-topped but many were later fitted with top covers, and new trams were ordered complete with these. But pity the poor driver! On many early cars there was no protection either in front or above him. Only a good overcoat and cap would save him from the elements. In time, better protection was incorporated and ultimately many trams were completely enclosed. Tram bodies were craftsman-built, often to the individual requirements of an operator; thus there was an infinite number of variations in design.

Criticism

When war broke out in 1914, trams were summoned to even greater service. Many buses were commandeered, and trams became overloaded. There was a shortage of men and materials to carry out repairs to vehicles, track and overhead. When war ended, many tramway systems were in a sorry state. Although the days of electric trams were far from over, criticism began to increase. Trams were inflexible; they caused congestion on busy roads. Motor buses were becoming larger and more reliable. The trolleybus was now a force to be reckoned with. The

7. Shown here at Swinton Common, a few miles north of Rotherham, is tram no. 13 of the Mexborough and Swinton Tramway Co. Operation was by the surface contact system. The metal studs can be seen between the tracks in this view. Length of skate beneath the car and spacing of studs were such that the skate contacted the next stud before breaking contact with the previous one. Beneath the studs was the continuous power cable. Dirty road conditions and wet weather sometimes lead to erratic functioning of the studs which caused electric shocks to people and horses. In general, the surface contact system was a failure. Tramways which used it were, after varying periods, converted to overhead wiring. Card no. 978 by C.F. Hurst.

first electric tramway abandonment was at Sheerness, Kent, in 1917. During the middle and late 'twenties, several systems, mostly relatively small, ceased to exist. Nevertheless, the number of trams operating reached a peak in 1927 with almost 14,500 vehicles in operation. Some cities and towns still had faith in their trams.

Abandonments
During the nineteen-thirties, approximately 125 tramway undertakings were abandoned. Through the 1939-45 war, many systems which would, under normal circumstances, have succumbed, soldiered on. By the end of hostilities, much track and many trams were in poor condition. Some modern trams were built after the war, including those at Aberdeen, Glasgow and Sheffield. What never seemed to materialise were proper inter-urban schemes with modern single-deck railcars. With increased running costs and many other problems, the end was drawing near. Some of the last systems to go had, in their heyday, been the largest, for example London (abandoned 1952), Liverpool (1957), Sheffield (1960) and Glasgow (1962). Blackpool, though, still has its trams and its plans for the future.

Golden Age
The real Golden Age of Tramways was from the turn of the century to the beginning of the 1914-18 war. This coincided with the great picture postcard era, and many of the cards reproduced in this book are from that period. They show how trams looked, where they went, and a myriad of other interesting features to the discerning eye.

Contents

HORSE TRAMS

8. The Exeter Tramways Co. Ltd. operated horse trams from 1882 onwards. Single-deck and double-deck cars were used, one of the latter being shown. The lady upstairs had established herself on the knifeboard-type seating. The position of the people in the lower saloon indicates that the seating was longitudinal. The tramway was acquired by Exeter Corporation in 1903 and electrified, with extensions, in 1905-6. The view probably originates from that period because a pole and bracket arm for electric traction have been erected, right. Card by Cumming and Co., Exeter.

9. The Morecambe Tramways Co. operated a horse tramway from Strawberry Gardens, Heysham to East View, Morecambe. The section from Battery Inn to East View, part of which is illustrated, was purchased by Morecambe Corporation in 1908 and extended to Bare. This was the last horse tramway in mainland England when it closed in 1926. The tram shown could carry 22 passengers inside and 26 outside, according to a notice on its end. An advert on the side exhorted holidaymakers to *'Visit the Winter Gardens, 6d'*. Card posted from Morecambe, 11th July 1914.

10. This card shows a Clapton-bound horse tram of the Lea Bridge, Leyton and Walthamstow Tramways Co. at the Bakers Arms, Leyton. Some of the intending passengers may have been in the public house, left, or in the many shops which lined the street (butcher, baker, ironmonger, to name a few). Tram services were operated between the Rising Sun Inn near Epping Forest and Clapton, with a branch, right foreground, to Leyton Station. 'Rotary' postcard by Hawkins, stationer, High Road, Leyton.

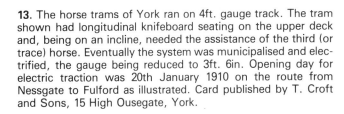

11. This Lincoln memorial card is largely self-explanatory. Driver George Pimp was the bowler-hatted gentleman fourth from left. The phrase *'Succumbed to an electric shock'* was a favourite on this type of card, where electric trams replaced their horse counterparts. T.G.H. series printed card.

Mr. GEORGE PIMP the Driver of the FIRST CAR in 1882, the LAST CAR on 22nd July, 1905.

In Affectionate Remembrance
OF THE
LINCOLN HORSE CARS
which succumbed to an Electric Shock, after years of faithful service,
22nd July, 1905.
"GONE BUT NOT FORGOTTEN."

12. Horse trams were operated in Oxford from 1882 onwards by the City of Oxford and District Tramways Co. Ltd. In 1906, a new company, the City of Oxford Electric Tramways Ltd., was formed with a view to converting to electric traction. Indecision as to the type of electric system to adopt caused the horse cars to drag on for another seven years. They were eventually replaced by motor-buses in 1913-14. Card postmarked Oxford, 18th February 1914.

13. The horse trams of York ran on 4ft. gauge track. The tram shown had longitudinal knifeboard seating on the upper deck and, being on an incline, needed the assistance of the third (or trace) horse. Eventually the system was municipalised and electrified, the gauge being reduced to 3ft. 6in. Opening day for electric traction was 20th January 1910 on the route from Nessgate to Fulford as illustrated. Card published by T. Croft and Sons, 15 High Ousegate, York.

STEAM TRAMS

8657

14. This view of a steam tram engine and passenger trailer of the North London Tramways Co. was taken sometime before 1891, when the system was acquired by the North Metropolitan Tramways Co. for horse tram operation. The card (no. 8657) was published some years later by F. Moore of 3 Amen Corner, London, who was more usually associated with railway photographs. The engine, built by Merryweather, had a roof condenser, from where condensed steam was returned to the feed-water tank.

Retired From Active Service June 1904

15. One of the largest steam tram undertakings was the Manchester, Bury, Rochdale and Oldham Steam Tramway. Eventually the routes were purchased by various corporations and urban district councils with a view to electrification. Heywood, because of failure to agree with neighbours Bury and Rochdale, found itself without trams of any kind in June 1904. The problem was partly solved some months later when Heywood purchased some redundant steam tram engines and trailers from Rochdale. The revived service was short-lived; following a subsequent agreement with Rochdale for the running of electric trams, the Heywood steam service ceased on 20th September 1905. The card, which shows a Heywood and Hopwood route tram, was posted from Heywood on 25th September 1905, but, if the hand-written caption on the front is correct, the view related to the earlier withdrawal.

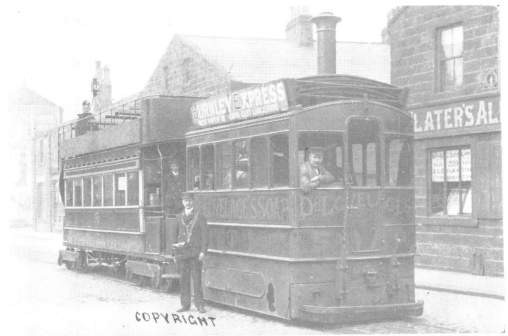

16. An advert for the 'Burnley Express' on the side of the engine is the clue to the identity of this combination, operated by the Burnley and District Tramways Co. Ltd. Hardly visible lower down was an advert for Dr. Lovelace's Soap, the use of which may have been a necessity after a ride on top of the trailer! Track gauge for the steam trams was 4ft. 8½in., reduced to 4ft. on electrification.

17. This could be described as a tram graveyard. It shows the breaking-up of the Accrington steam trams. The box-like casing had been removed from the foremost engine and revealed some similarity with a small railway locomotive. The name 'Baltic Fleet' was said to derive from the resemblance between the tram engines and the ships of the Russian Baltic Fleet which attacked the British fishing fleet in the North Sea in 1904.

End Of Accrington's "Baltic Fleet" July 1907.

The Train, Mumbles. No 8334.

18. The Swansea and Mumbles Railway (Oystermouth Railway) is usually regarded as the precursor of both the passenger railway and tramway. Although called a railway, it had many features of a tramway. Originally horse-operated, steam engines were introduced in 1877. The locomotive illustrated was built by the Hunslet Engine Co. in 1899. The passenger vehicles behind the loco resembled early tramcars. Electrification occurred in 1929 when mammoth all-enclosed trams which seated 106 people were introduced. Closure came in 1960.

TRACK LAYING

19. The Birmingham steam tram network was the most extensive in Britain, very complex, and operated by the Birmingham and Aston Tramways Co. Ltd., Birmingham and Midland Tramways Ltd., Birmingham Central Tramways Co. Ltd. and later the City of Birmingham Tramways Co. Ltd. Horse trams were in the minority and operated on only three routes. This card shows laying of wood blocks between the tracks at Smallheath in connection with electrification of the Coventry Road line of the C.B.T. Co. Ltd. (a British Electric Traction Co. Ltd. subsidiary) in 1905. By 1911 Birmingham Corporation had taken over all company operation. Card by Percy Wynne, 518 Coventry Road, Smallheath.

20. This card shows re-laying of the tramway during conversion from steam to electric operation in 1905 at Smallbridge on the Rochdale to Littleborough route. Workers and watchers were photographed against a background of typical Pennine-fringe buildings.

21. Track of 3ft. 6in. gauge is shown being laid in Queen's Road for the Hastings Tramways Co., whose electric cars began operation on 31st July 1905. Hastings never had horse trams; the appearance of lines in the road would be a novelty worthy of a postcard; this one was in the J.O. Forster (of Queen's Road) series.

DELIVERIES

22. The message on this card, posted from Accrington to Carnforth on 27th July 1907 is *'My dear mother, I hope you won't fret about me going away to Canada. I will look after myself and will return to you again by and by. I shall not be able to see the cars start.'* Accrington Corporation operated electric trams from 2nd August 1907 after taking over part of the local steam tramway company. For the opening, four single-deck and fourteen double-deck trams were ordered from the Brush Electrical Engineering Co. Ltd., Loughborough. Following delivery to the nearest railway sidings, they were taken to the tram depot on low wagons pulled by horses. Here, tram no. 3 is seen arriving at the depot minus trucks which had been removed for the journey from Loughborough.

23. This card merely has the caption *'Tram arriving'*. Faintly indented on the back is the photographer's name 'Walker, 28 Wood Street, Wakefield'. A magnifying glass reveals the crest of the Wakefield and District Light Railway Co., later the Yorkshire (West Riding) Electric Tramways Co. Ltd. The tram shown, no. 24, had been built at the Electric Railway and Tramway Carriage Works Ltd., Preston (note the window bill). It arrived at Belle Isle Depot, Wakefield, on a low-loader pulled by a traction engine. Final fitting of upper-deck seats, panels and handrails, plus trolley standards and destination indicators, was done at the depot.

OPENINGS

24. Horse trams operated in Gloucester from 1879. The system was purchased by Gloucester Corporation in 1902 for subsequent electrification which included conversion from 4ft. to 3ft. 6in. gauge. This view, outside the Avenue Hotel, shows the electric car trial-run on 5th April 1904, a month before the official tramway opening. All thirty electric trams in the fleet, including no. 1 shown, were constructed by the Brush Electrical Engineering Co. Ltd. of Loughborough. Card by Pitcher, postmarked Gloster (note spelling) 8th April 1904 (three days after the event).

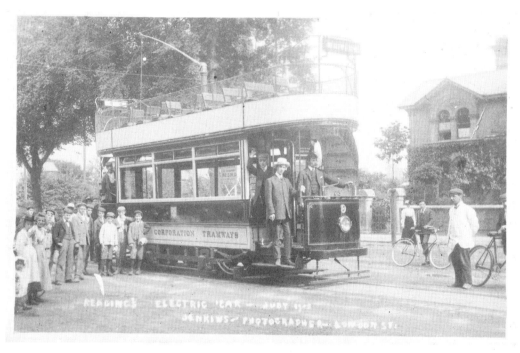

25. A posed shot taken in July 1903 at the opening of the Reading electric trams. Horse cars had operated from 1879, the system was municipalised in 1901 and electric trams worked from 1903 until they were gradually scrapped during the 1930's. All cars were built at the Electric Railway and Tramway Carriage Works Ltd., Preston, and the gauge was 4ft. On abandonment, some routes were converted to trolleybus operation. Card by Jenkins, London Street.

26. The location: outside the Town Hall, High Street, Colchester. The occasion: the opening by the mayoress of the electric tramway on 28th July 1904. The weather: some rain, if the umbrellas are any guide. The mood: happy and joyous. The card, by W. Gill of Colchester, was posted from there on 30th July 1904, two days after the opening.

27. A crowded scene (approximately eighty people) at the opening of the small 4ft. 8½in. gauge electric tramway of Lincoln Corporation on 23rd November 1905. The cars were operated by the Griffiths-Bedell stud surface contact system, which explains the absence of any overhead impedimenta. From 1919 onwards, the system was changed to overhead current supply.

28. Horse trams of the Keighley Tramways Co. Ltd. were taken over by Keighley Corporation in 1901 and replaced by electric trams in 1904. Keighley twice used trolleybuses; from 1913 to 1921 during its tramway era and from 1924 to 1932 as replacements for its trams. Car no. 8 was photographed at Utley on the first day of operation. This and other trams in the fleet were built by Brush of Loughborough.

29. Two views for the price of one on this card of the opening of Northampton's electric trams. The new cars already carried advertisements on their upper deck sides, some for Kendall's umbrellas. The same item was advertised in a shop window on the left in the upper view. The summer shadows and the dress of the crowds suggest the day was fine and that umbrellas would not be needed.

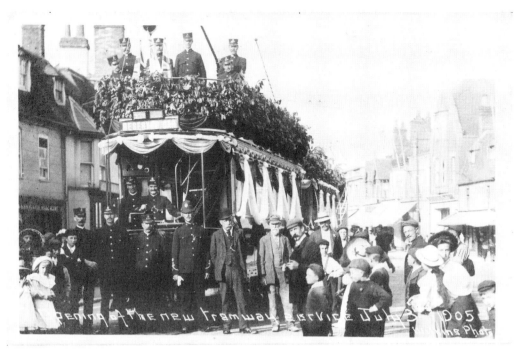

30. Bournemouth's sizeable 3ft. 6in. gauge electric tramway eventually stretched west to Poole and east to Christchurch. Westwards, trams originally ran to County Gates where Hampshire and Dorset met. The Poole and District Electric Traction Co. (a British Electric Traction Co. Ltd. subsidiary) operated a tramway from there to Poole. This was purchased by Bournemouth Corporation in June 1905 and the sixteen trams numbered into the Bournemouth fleet. Apart from one single-decker, all Bournemouth trams (including Poole acquisitions) were open-top double-deckers throughout their life. The gap in the rails at County Gates was joined and through running commenced on 3rd July 1905. The opening of the through service was depicted on this view at Poole. Trams were withdrawn between 1929 and 1936, most routes becoming trolleybus-operated. Photo by Wilkins, postmarked Poole, 7th July 1905.

31. Running east-west for about five miles just north of the Firth of Tay were the tracks of the Dundee, Broughty Ferry and District Tramways Co. Ltd. These stretched from Monifieth through Broughty Ferry to the outskirts of Dundee to join those of Dundee Corporation. Three cars were decorated with red, white and blue bunting for the inaugural ceremony. The illustration shows one at Monifieth terminus on opening day, 27th December 1905. With open upper decks and no driver protection, these cars were rather out-dated when built in 1905, having been modelled on similar Preston-built cars on the Dundee Corporation system. They were the only trams built by Brush to this design.

32. Famous for its coal, the Rhondda Valley had the most extensive tramway layout in South Wales, running through places with such names as Treorchy, Trehafod and Treherbert. It was opened by the Rhondda Tramways Co. Ltd., a member of the National Electric Construction Co. Ltd. group. Shown here is the first tram in Tonypandy on 29th October 1908. Card postmarked Ynishir (near Tonypandy) November 1908.

STREET SCENES

High Street, Kirkcaldy.

33. Tram No.6 is shown on single 3ft. 6in. gauge track in High Street, Kirkcaldy, a town on the north bank of the Firth of Forth. Trams were operated from 28th February 1903 to 15th May 1931, when Kirkcaldy Corporation accepted an offer from W. Alexander and Sons Ltd. of £27,000, and £2,000 a year for 21 years to operate motorbuses. Card published by Valentine and Sons Ltd., Dundee, about twenty miles further north.

Lower Briggate,

34. Local Leeds firm W. and T. Gaines produced this view of Lower Briggate, Leeds. On the extreme left is the shop of Dyson and Sons, jewellers, which still stands in the same position. In front of Leeds Corporation tram no. 185, Lower Briggate became Briggate, which today is even busier than ever.

35. H. Burt, stationer, of Chorlton published this card of one of Manchester Corporation's single-deck cars. They could be seen on the well-known circular route to the north, east and south of the city (eventually called route 53) which ran along narrow, winding streets and under low railway bridges. Tram no. 534, which is shown at Seymour Grove terminus, was part of the 512-536 batch introduced in 1903. It was known as a combination car because of its central saloon (which seated 28 passengers on longitudinal seats) and open smoking compartments at each end (each of which seated passengers on crossbench seats). Card posted from Chorlton-cum-Hardy, 14th July 1906.

WEST POINT, CHORLTON-CUM-HARDY.

36. Tramways of Newcastle-upon-Tyne were always municipally owned, although in horse tram days leased to the Newcastle and Gosforth Tramways and Carriage Co. Ltd. Electrification was carried out from 1901-4. The last trams ran on 4th March 1950, though some track was used by the Gateshead and District Tramways Co. for a further seventeen months.

Many routes underwent conversion to trolleybus operation. Newcastle Corporation had a varied selection of single-deck and double-deck trams on its extensive 4ft 8½in gauge system. This scene in Northumberland Street shows all-enclosed car no. 279 which was new in 1923, car no. 125 which was bought in 1901 as an open-topper and, furthest away, a former single-decker, new in 1901, which was one of a batch rebuilt with short upper decks and nicknamed 'submarines'. Posted from Hebburn, 27th May 1928.

37. This car was no. 44 in the fleet of the Stalybridge, Hyde, Mossley and Dukinfield Tramways and Electricity Board, which represented those four local authorities with tramway operations. The Board's trams also ran into Ashton-under-Lyne where they mingled with those of Ashton, Manchester and Oldham Corporations (an Ashton Corporation car can be seen in the background). The S.H.M.D. ceased to operate trams in 1945 although some tracks continued in use by Manchester and Stockport Corporations until 1947. Card no. 02431 by E. Lumb, Ashton-under-Lyne.

38. Not far from Doncaster town centre, the then new bridge over the Great Northern Railway carried tram no. 2, bound for the racecourse on a cross-town service. The car was new in 1902. Doncaster Corporation abandoned its trams in 1928-35, mostly in favour of trolleybuses. Card by Regina Co., press photographers, Doncaster, posted from there on 2nd May 1913.

39. Three operators' services met in the centre of Rotherham. On this view of College Square, all are represented. In front is a Sheffield Corporation car, next two Rotherham Corporation cars, with a Mexborough and Swinton Tramways Co. car at the back. This postcard, no. 172-93, came from E.L. Scrivens of Doncaster, who produced fine photographic and often superbly-animated views of Doncaster and surrounding areas.

40. The Potteries Electric Traction Co. Ltd. (a British Electric Traction Co. Ltd. subsidiary) had the largest all-single-deck tram fleet in the British Isles. 31 miles 58 chains of 4ft. gauge tramway covered several towns in the Stoke-on-Trent and Hanley area. Part of the system was leased from the North Staffordshire Tramways Co. Ltd. There were four-wheel and eight-wheel bogie cars and the fleet numbers reached 125. Some early cars were withdrawn and replaced by new cars with the same numbers. Others were rebuilt and re-numbered. This lively view shows a tram of the Potteries Company at Longton, south-east of Stoke. Postcard no. 295-1 from the Doncaster Rotophoto Co. Ltd.

41. A car of the Dunfermline and District Tramways Co. at the Park Gates, Dunfermline, on a Davidson's Scotch Design series card.

42. Newcastle-upon-Tyne Corporation trams outside the railway station (right) in Neville Street on an 'Art Colour' postcard, no. A1220, from an original watercolour by G.W. Blow, published by Valentines of Dundee.

43. Tram no. 2 of the Barnsley and District Electric Traction Co. Ltd. in Sheffield Road, Barnsley. Card by W.C. Machan, Kirkgate, Wakefield, postmarked Wombwell on 13th July 1908.

44. A pair of City of Hull Tramways cars in tree-lined Spring Bank. Card no. 20296 of Blum and Degen's 'Kromo' series, London.

45. In Plumstead at the time of changeover from horse to electric traction: a horse car of the Woolwich and South East London Tramways Co. Ltd. stands in front of its successor, an electric tram of the London County Council. Card by Wilson and Sons, Printers, Woolwich.

46. Trams of the London County Council in Kennington Park Road just south of the Thames. Stengel and Co. card no. E25478.

47. Tram no. 5 of the Gravesend and Northfleet Electric Tramways Ltd. (of the B.E.T. group) at St. James' Church, Gravesend. There were ten of these cars. They were rather large for Gravesend and, after four years there, were transferred to other B.E.T. undertakings. Photochrom card no. 23150.

48. Two trams in the Market Place, Nottingham, by artist Charles E. Flower on a Tuck 'Oilette' postcard (series no. 1783).

BY THE SEA

49. A crossbench (covered toastrack) tram amongst holidaymakers at Ettrick Bay on the Scottish Isle of Bute. The system of the Rothesay Tramways Co. Ltd. included reserved sleeper track across the island from Port Bannatyne to Ettrick Bay.

50. At Dunluce Castle, County Antrim, two cars of the Giant's Causeway, Portrush and Bush Valley Railway and Tramway Co., whose lines ran from Portrush to Bushmills and later to near Giant's Causeway. Originally steam, then third-rail electrically operated, the system was eventually converted to overhead wiring. It survived until 1949. Card by W. Lawrence, Dublin.

51. Cars of the Great Grimsby Street Tramways Co. in Cleethorpes Road, Grimsby, famous for its fish. Not quite the seaside, but this company did operate trams into the adjoining resort of Cleethorpes. Card by Valentines of Dundee, no. 28302.

52. Not a tram in sight, but an interesting view of the tram station at Ramsey (Isle of Man), the northern terminus of the 3ft. gauge Manx Electric Railway from Douglas. Reliable Series card no. R.235 by William Ritchie and Sons Ltd., Edinburgh.

53. A chromo-litho postcard to celebrate the opening of the first section of Weston-super-Mare pier on 11th June 1904, and which includes two trams.

54. Cars 24 and 40 of Brighton Corporation at the southern end of Victoria Gardens, Brighton. This terminus was later projected southwards to Old Steine, quite near to Magnus Volk's tramway. E.W.B. card, series 1.

55. At Royal Parade, Ramsgate, a tram of the Isle of Thanet Electric Supply Co. Ltd., whose single route connected the resorts of Margate, Broadstairs and Ramsgate. The card, from the Milton 'Artlette' series no. 160, of Woolstone Brothers, London is enhanced or defiled, depending on taste, by the addition of 'glitter'.

49 Ettrick Bay, Bute.

50 Dunluce Castle Co. Antrim.

Cleethorpes Road, Grimsby

51

Ramsey Tram Station I.O.M. 52

Weston-super-Mare Grand Pier & Pavilion

53 First Section opened June 11th 1904.

The Trams and Victoria Gardens   Brighton

54

Royal Parade   Ramsgate

55

56. Lytham St. Annes had its own tramway, operated by the Blackpool, St. Annes and Lytham Tramways Co. Ltd. which later passed to St. Annes Urban District Council and finally to Lytham St. Annes Corporation. The trams, which ran into Blackpool, were replaced by buses in 1936-37. In addition to conventional trams, the fleet included 20 unusual double-deck cars with open-sided lower decks, two of which are shown here at Lytham.

P.C. 41736 Llandudno & Colwyn Bay Tramway, At Sunny Hill.

57. The Llandudno and Colwyn Bay Electric Railway Ltd. operated a long tramway route from Llandudno West Shore, through Llandudno, past Little Orme, through Rhos-on-Sea and Colwyn Bay to Old Colwyn. Track was along built-up streets and through fields, as seen here at Sunny Hill. Two of the original 1907 cars are shown. With an injection of second-hand single-deckers from Accrington and double-deckers from Bournemouth, much of the tramway survived into the 'fifties. Two modern streamlined double-deck cars were bought from Darwen, but M.O.T. regulations forbade their use on the exposed stretches of line. They provided shuttle services in Llandudno and Colwyn Bay. In 1956, track condition and bus competition caused complete closure. Photochrom Glossy Photo series no. P.C.41736, posted from Llandudno, 8th September 1910.

58. Great Yarmouth Corporation operated 3ft. 6in. gauge tramways on each side of the River Yare; a narrow swing bridge prevented any connection. The southern part ran to Gorleston and closed in 1930. The northern part, which ran to Caister, was abandoned in 1925 and 1933. All 35 trams were four-wheel open-toppers. The 25 bodies used north of the river ended their career at Caister Holiday Camp. This view at Hall Quay, Great Yarmouth, shows car no. 2 which presumably became a 'camp conscript'.

59. The Hastings Tramways Co. had routes in the town itself, a circular rural route to the north and a long route along the coast through St. Leonards and Bexhill to Cooden. Until 1914, the coastal section between Hastings Memorial and St. Leonards West Marina used the Dolter stud surface contact system of current collection. This view at St. Leonards shows the junction of the tracks from Silverhill, right, which had overhead wiring. The tram's trolley arm was hooked in the down position because current was being picked up through the road studs. Just visible, suspended from the fender of the tram, between the lines, is a short-circuiting device in case the stud remained live after the skate under the car had passed over it. Card by F.N. Broderick, Ryde, Isle of Wight.

60. The 3ft. 6in. gauge of Southend-on-Sea Corporation Tramways is emphasised by the rear view of this tram and its projecting upper deck. Car no. 45 was photographed in Broadway, Leigh-on-Sea, at the eastern end of the system. Behind the motor-car in the centre, a man on a tower-wagon is shown attending to a tram pole. Jarrolds of Norwich card no. J.9072.

61. Portsmouth Corporation operated a busy compact system in the Portsmouth/Southsea/Copnor/Cosham area. The track gauge, like that of two nearby systems (at Gosport/Fareham and in the Portsdown/Horndean area) was the unusual 4ft. 7¾in. There are many cards of Southsea Common; this Louis Levy printed card, no. 30, is one of the better examples.

30 SOUTHSEA. — The Common. — LL.

STREET SCENES

62. Published by Lawrence of Dublin, this view shows Shaftesbury Square, Belfast. The style of printing on the card ensured that the tram tracks were given prominence. The many routes of Belfast's large municipal system radiated from the city centre. Fifty luxurious modern trams were introduced as late as 1935 but the whole network was switched to trolleybuses and motor-buses between 1938 and 1954.

63. F.G.O. Stuart of Southampton primarily published viewcards of Hampshire. This example, no. 407, captioned 'Above Bar, Southampton' shows an early open-top tram passing the clock tower which eventually was moved to another location. Virtually everything else shown on the card has vanished. The last tram ran in Southampton in 1949.

64. Narrow Ipswich streets dictated a track gauge of 3ft. 6in. and trams of only 5ft. 9in. width. They were replaced by trolleybuses in 1923-26. The card is from Raphael Tuck 'Oilette' series 7146; the artist is not stated. Trams featured only infrequently on the vast number of 'Oilette' and similar Tuck postcards and were rarely as prominent as this.

65. The Norwich Electric Tramways Co. was never municipalised; control eventually passed to the Eastern Counties Omnibus Co. who abandoned the tramway for motorbuses in 1935. This card was posted in 1931 and the view dates from then or a few years before. The signs of the Mann Egerton Garage on the left proclaimed *'Garage for 500 cars open always'* and *'250 new and used cars'*. An indication of the style of transport in the future and an omen for the trams! Card by Jarrolds of Norwich, no. J.9197.

66. Ten companies, most of which originated as horse tram operators, were purchased between 1895 and 1909 by London County Council to form the core of the London tramway network. The L.C.C. electric system differed from most others in Britain because it operated mainly on the conduit principle. A plough beneath the tramcar passed along a slot, seen in this view. Shoes on the end of the plough made contact with two conductor rails in the conduit beneath the slot. L.C.C. tram no. 257 was caught passing the South-Eastern Railway Station in New Cross Road, on its way to Greenwich via Old Kent Road. Card by Perkins and Sons, Lewisham.

67. Apart from London, the largest tramway system in the British Isles belonged to Glasgow Corporation, which, together with surrounding company systems, formed a huge network. All had the unusual 4ft. 7¾in. gauge to enable railway wagons to use the tram tracks. For many years, the streets of Glasgow were brightened by the unique tramcar livery. Lower-deck window frames were cream; upper-deck ones were brown. Lower-deck end and side panels were orange but those around the upper-deck were red, blue, green, yellow or white, depending on the route. The scene at the junction of Argyle Street and Union Street includes five Glasgow 'caurs'. Some plans for tramway modernisation materialised. In the late 'forties, there were still 1200 cars. Ideas and plans changed. The last trams ran in 1962.

68. The Electric Supply Corporation Ltd. opened a small tramway system in Dumbarton in 1907. This was later purchased by the Dumbarton Burgh and County Tramways Co. Ltd., who considerably extended two of the routes. One extension ran to Balloch on Loch Lomond, the other to Dalmuir West where there was an end-on junction with the Clydebank Tramways, later owned by Glasgow Corporation. Renton, shown on this postcard, was on the route to the 'Bonnie Banks'. Card published by W. Love, stationer, Glasgow, postally used 1913.

MAIN STREET, RENTON, NO. 1

6433   KILMARNOCK. DUKE STREET.   ROTARY PHOTO E.C.

69. About twenty miles south-west of Glasgow, Kilmarnock Corporation operated three short routes of 4ft. 8½in. gauge tramway with only fourteen cars, no. 1 of which is shown here in Duke Street. Opened in 1904, the tramway lasted a little over twenty years and was one of the first to be abandoned. Card no. 6433, published by Rotary Photographic Co. Ltd. from a photo by William Ritchie, Edinburgh.

70. From 1898, electric trams in Cork, Southern Ireland, were operated by the Cork Electric Tramways and Lighting Co. Ltd. Unusually, the gauge was 2ft. 11½in. because of the original intention, which came to naught, to run through coaches from two adjacent light railways. The narrowness of the gauge can be seen on this card of Patrick Street, from which the various routes radiated. Buses replaced the trams in 1931.. Valentines of Dundee card no. 98510.

71. After horse trams which ceased in 1901, Newport Corporation (Monmouthshire) operated a varied fleet of double-deck electric trams. *'All cars stop here'* read a notice on the pole. Tram no. 32 had stopped by the side of a horse-drawn bread van at Stow Hill. The preponderance of people on the car's upper deck and the short shadows suggest it was a warm summer day.

72. Framed by Clarence Bridge (the date on top is 1890) is car no. 16 of Cardiff Corporation. Note the interlaced track on the bridge. The Corporation system was based upon two horse tramways which were taken over and electrified early in the century. Cardiff introduced a pay-as-you-enter method in the 'forties with a universal 1d fare and no tickets issued. Trolleybus replacement started in 1942; the last trams ran in 1950. Posted from Cardiff, 31st August 1911.

73. Derby Corporation acquired the horse routes of the Derby Tramways Co. Ltd. in 1899, electrified them in 1904 and opened further routes in the following few years. Routes generally radiated from the town centre, the longer ones being to the south. Car no. 7, of the first batch of electric trams purchased, is seen in busy Victoria Street. Trams were replaced by trolleybuses in 1932-34. Card no. 289/25 in the 'Reliable' series of William Ritchie and Sons Ltd., Edinburgh.

74. The 1902 Bill of the Nottinghamshire and Derbyshire Tramways Co. asked for 79 miles of route. Eventually only one route was constructed, 11⅜ miles long, which was opened in 1913. Trams ran from Ripley to Cinderhill and then over Nottingham Corporation tracks into that city. Here, tram no. 20, bound for Nottingham, is on single-track at Ripley. Card postally used from Ripley on 29th July 1919.

75. Tram no. 44 of Wolverhampton Corporation was caught passing the Empire Palace at the end of Victoria Street in the centre of Wolverhampton. The absence of poles and overhead wires was due to operation by the Lorain stud surface contact system. This was changed to overhead current collection in 1921. Wolverhampton eventually became a trolleybus stronghold. John Price and Sons real photo series.

76. Coventry Corporation purchased the already electrified routes of the Coventry Electric Tramways Co. in 1912. The southern parts of the system were abandoned in 1932-37. At the outbreak of the 1939 war, two routes remained and a third was re-opened to save liquid fuel. The German air-raid of 14th November 1940 left craters in the roads and extensively damaged the feeder cables. This lead to swift abandonment of the remains of the system. In this between-the-wars view (taken at twenty minutes to four in the afternoon according to the two clocks), motor transport is predominant. TC (Teesee) series card no. 399.

77. The Bath Electric Tramways Ltd. operated six routes in the historic city. In 1936, control passed to the Bristol Tramways and Carriage Co. Ltd. whose own extensive system was not far away. The Bath system was abandoned in 1938-39. Here, tram no. 26, new in 1904, is shown in Kingsmead Square. Louis Levy printed card no. 77.

SUBURBAN OR SYLVAN

78. This card shows Devonshire Terrace, Stanwix, and was produced by Porthouse of Carlisle. Stanwix is approximately one mile north of Carlisle centre. The system of the City of Carlisle Electric Tramway Co. Ltd. was isolated, being fifty miles from any other tramway. Three single-deck and twelve double-deck cars, including no. 8 shown here, were purchased in 1900 but withdrawn in 1912, a relatively short life for tramcars. They were replaced by up-to-date trams.

Herrington Burn. 3690

79. Herrington Burn, shown on this 'Monarch' series card published by R. Johnston and Son, Gateshead, was several miles south-west of Sunderland. The tram belonged to the Sunderland District Electric Tramways, an inter-urban single-track system (with passing loops) which went through a series of colliery towns and villages and was a separate entity to Sunderland Corporation Tramways. A financial failure, it closed down in 1925. In this view, the conductress has wandered some yards to the right for a chat and the driver is posed behind the tram's controls, accompanied by some of the local people who, even if cloth-capped, appear well-dressed.

80. A tram ride to the park would be an experience enjoyed in many towns. Preston Corporation car no. 24 is seen at Moor Park Lodge, Garstang Road, on the circular route via Fulwood. Preston was renowned for tramcar construction, many thousands being built at the famous works of Dick, Kerr and Co. Ltd. on the western edge of the town. The Electric Railway and Tramway Carriage Works Ltd., and later the United Electric Car Co. Ltd., were part of the Dick, Kerr complex at Preston. Card by Winter of Preston.

81. Cars of the Yorkshire (West Riding) Electric Tramways Co. Ltd. operated on three routes. These were from Leeds through Lofthouse and Wakefield to Sandal, from Ossett through Horbury and Wakefield to Agbrigg and (isolated from the other two) from Normanton through Castleford to Pontefract. Although Benton Hill shown here was just a short distance from Horbury town centre, it had a somewhat rural appearance. This card emanated from 28 Wood Street, Wakefield (refer illustration no. 23) but the photographer's name had changed to Wilson.

82. The Leamington and Warwick Electrical Co. Ltd. had a three-mile long tramway of 3ft. 6in. gauge which ran between those towns. Thirteen electric cars were operated from 1905 to 1930. No. 1 is seen here crossing Victoria Bridge, Leamington Spa, surrounded by leafy trees and other forms of transport which befit a spa town. Pelham series card by Boots Cash Chemists.

83. The towns of Devonport and Plymouth were served by a complicated network of tramways which belonged to three different operators, including Plymouth Corporation (which eventually absorbed the other two). Here, Plymouth Corporation tram no. 12, new in 1900, was caught in a decidedly sylvan setting at Compton Lane End, Plymouth (the caption is at right-angles to the view). Card no. 1971 in Muckamores series, Laira, postmarked Plymouth 3rd October 1906.

DECORATED TRAMS

84. Salford Corporation decorated this car for the visit of King Edward VII and Queen Alexandra on 12th July 1905. Visible on the tram are a bust of the King (at the end) and the words *'God save our noble King'* (on the side). The opposite end and side carried a bust of the Queen and the words *'God bless our gracious Queen'*. Some of the lights flashed on and off. Boden series card no. 494.

86. Dartford Urban District Council owned this car (fleet no. 12 is just visible) and decorated it for the 1911 Coronation. The depot and all the trams, including this one, were destroyed by fire in 1917. Photographed and published by F. Kehrhahn and Co., Bexleyheath.

85. Coronation Day. The Decorated Car. But where? The postcard is unused and has no publisher information. Virtually the only clues to identification are in the types of trams, the coat of arms on the front of the first one and the phrase *'Doncaster's best'* just readable on the side of the second. Research revealed that the decorations were hiding Doncaster Corporation car no. 21.

87. In the September 1925 Charity Carnival, Middlesbrough Corporation used this decorated tram to help raise money for local hospitals. A side window included the words *'Every penny helps'*. A penny would be worth something then! Originally a double-decker, the car had been converted to single-deck condition in 1911.

88. Little evidence of tram is visible here. The design was intended to encourage the war effort in Scarborough. The postmark includes the slogan *'Feed the Guns with War Bonds'* and is dated 12th November 1918, the day after the armistice. The message includes the phrase *'Got my Xmas cake this a.m.'* The resort had trams from 1904 to 1931, operated by the Scarborough Tramways Co., the gauge being 3ft. 6in.

89. In 1925, a Bristol tram was decorated as Noah's Ark and reminded people to support the Lord Mayor's Fund for Children's Christmas Dinners. Lit up, it would look attractive on the streets of Bristol just before Christmas.

90. This tram was decorated for Blackburn Show Week in November 1909. The temptation to obscure the car was resisted. The result: a good view of single-deck bogie tram no. 84. Posted from Blackburn on 2nd December 1909, the message is about visits to the Palace and Grand Theatres to see Variety and Sherlock Holmes respectively. Did they go by tram?

91. Although this car was decorated to promote Bradford Shopping Week in 1925, the design had a definite royal appearance. The explanation? This was a thinly-disguised re-hash of a design which had been used for the 1911 Coronation. The campaign may not have been a huge success, because the twenties were hardly years of affluence for many people. Card no. 4472 by Matthews of Bradford, well-known locally.

92. This card has the following message on the reverse (including spelling mistakes!) *'Dear Fred, Hoping you will like this postcard this his a special car for the French men when they was in Keighley. Hoping you all will enjoy yourself at the Feast and also have nice weather'.* The card must have been sent in an envelope because it carries no address or stamp.

OVERHEAD

93. The standards which supported the overhead wires were of several basic designs. One method was steel poles on each side of the road, with span wires between them which had hangers and ears for supporting the main wires. The view of Pier Terrace, Lowestoft, shows this method just beyond the tram. Nearer, a different system is shown which needed poles at only one side of the road, with bracket arms which supported two wires for trams going in either direction. Decorative wrought-iron scrollwork was introduced on the standards.

94. In the centre of Burnley, the poles were in the middle of the road and had double bracket arms, each branch supporting a single live wire. There was ornate scrollwork. The poles also supported lamps, both on top and part way down. The track gauge of Burnley Corporation trams was 4ft. and this is emphasised by the double-deckers shown.

95. In Old Market Street, Bristol, the ornamental blacksmith's art is shown in the elaborate scrollwork on the standards. The poles between the tracks had double arms. The pole in the foreground had a single arm to take the wires around a corner. Some supported lamps and the one on the left had two signs which read *'Electric cars stop here'*. The trams shown are typical of those which operated in Bristol, with little alteration, from the end of the last century to the early 'forties. They belonged to the Bristol Tramways and Carriage Co. Ltd. This Company was reluctant to spend money on modernisation of a fleet which could have been compulsorily purchased by the Corporation. Posted from Bristol.

SHELTERS

96. Passenger shelters came in all shapes, sizes and designs. The lower saloon of a steam tram trailer ended its life as a tram shelter (left in this view) at Milnrow tram terminus, near Rochdale. The car on the right belonged to Rochdale Corporation.

97. In their heyday, trams seemed to dominate Briggate, the best-known street in Leeds. For part of its length, the centre of the road had covered tram shelters (commonly called barriers). Wet or fine, you waited there for a car. The second tram from the camera was bound for Roundhay. It carried headcode 3, allocated to the Roundhay route from 1929. This and the motor-cars probably date the view as early 'thirties. Card no. 105 of Bamforth and Co. Ltd., Holmfirth.

98. Matching the splendour of Matlock in Derbyshire was this attractive clock-crowned tram shelter which dated from 1899. The 3ft. 6in. gauge cable tramway, opened in 1893, operated up steep Matlock Bank for a total length of 0.62 miles. In the centre channel between the lines was a continuously moving cable. Jaws beneath the tram were tightened or loosened on to the cable by the driver to motivate or stop the car (assisted by brakes). There were three double-deck open-top eight-wheel cars. No. 1 is shown here. Closure came in 1927.

STAFF

10513-24   LONDON LIFE   L.C.C. TRAMCAR CONDUCTOR   ROTARY PHOTO, E.C.

99. This Rotary 'London Life' card, no. 10513-24, shows a London County Council tramcar conductor on the platform of his tram. Ticket punch machine, leather money bag and whistle are all visible.

100. A Liverpool Corporation conductor and driver are posed beside their tram, no ordinary vehicle. Between 1908 and 1911, a number of first-class cars were introduced in Liverpool. They were painted white and served the more prosperous suburbs until 1923. For travel in the lower saloon with its plush seats, a higher fare was charged.

101. Some tramway undertakings had a band or cricket team. Here, members of Brighton Corporation Tramways Band were photographed in the resort's Preston Park on 27th August 1908. Card no. 22 by Collograph Co., Grange Road, Hove.

ACCIDENTS

102. On the evening of 5th February 1916, Gateshead and District Tramways Co. single-deck car no. 7 was on a passing loop in Bensham Road. The lights of the oncoming car could be seen further up the hill. A pedestrian informed the driver of no. 7 that a fight was in progress on the other tram, so he applied his handbrake and walked up the hill to offer assistance. The conductress, unaware of his absence, allowed two dozen more people to board. The extra weight caused the tram to cascade 200 yards down the hill before it overturned, as seen here. Four pedestrians were killed and ten people in the car injured, some seriously.

103. On Saturday, 3rd March 1906, the driver experienced difficulty in starting Huddersfield Corporation tram no. 26 in Newsome Road and it began to run backwards down the hill. Narrowly missing a horse and cart, it finally derailed and stopped with its shocked passengers near a fish-and-chip shop. In this view, car no. 26 is in the background; car no. 35 in the foreground was used to place the damaged tram back on the tracks and move it to the depot. Postmarked Huddersfield, 22nd March 1906.

104. Although numbered in the Yorkshire (Woollen District) Electric Tramways Ltd. fleet, Batley Corporation owned eight trams, one of which had a mishap on 16th January 1904. Car no. 55 left the rails on a sharp curve at the corner of Thorncliffe Road and Track Road, Batley, crashed through a stone wall and ended, as seen here, in the grounds of a house. The driver and two passengers were injured. Two reports published later criticised the driver. The tram was renovated and renumbered no. 60, probably to allay superstitions.

105. This car, which belonged to the Stalybridge, Hyde, Mossley and Dukinfield Tramways and Electricity Board, went out of control on Ditchcroft Hill, Millbrook, on 2nd April 1908, careered downwards and landed in the river. It was pulled out with a traction engine and winding gear. This was one of three tram accidents on the same hill. Card by W. Hallas and Sons, 72 Market Street, Stalybridge.

106. Wallasey Corporation had five different types of four-wheel double-deck car operating on four distinct routes, each of which started and finished at the same New Brighton and Seacombe termini. One day, tram no. 36 had a mishap and came to rest on the pavement of Seabank Road between some houses and a small tree.

107. This accident occurred at Highgate, Middlesex, on 23rd June 1906. A car of the Metropolitan Electric Tramways Ltd. went out of control whilst descending Archway Road, collided with a bus and a hearse and came to rest after crashing into another tram which was standing at the terminus before departure for Whetstone. Both trams carried the names 'County Council of Middlesex' and 'Metropolitan Electric Tramways Ltd.' This was because the County Council insisted on their name being included on cars which ran on tracks which belonged to them but were leased to the Company.

108. The only tramway in Wiltshire was that of Swindon Corporation with 13 double-deck open-top cars of 3ft. 6in. gauge. On the evening of 1st June 1906, tram no. 11, well-filled with people, ran away down the steep gradient in Victoria Road, left the tracks on a curve near the town hall and ended on its side, as shown here. Four passengers were killed and thirty injured. Card by Hooper, photographer, Cromwell Street, Swindon, posted from Swindon on 1st October 1906.

109. Noted for coverage of events and disasters, Warner Gothard of Barnsley produced this interesting card of the Bournemouth tram accident. The car, carrying forty people, became out of control whilst descending Poole Hill (in Bournemouth), derailed on a curve and fell down a bank. Seven people were killed and many seriously injured. An enquiry revealed faulty brakes and the driver was exonerated from blame. Gothard cards are usually a combination of photographic images, art work (sometimes amateurish) and written details. This card has a photo of the driver. Next to him is a sketch of the crashed tram. Above that, the car is a mixture of photo and drawing. Each carries fleet no. 72. At the top, the street is taken from a photograph and the tram is a superimposed retouched photo. This has the stairway on the wrong side and fleet no. 52. Posted from Bournemouth, 17th July 1908.

MISCELLANY

110. Most tramway systems had engineering trams such as railgrinders or overhead maintenance vehicles. This solid-tyred lorry was used at Edinburgh for overhead repair work. Works vehicles such as this are rare on postcards.

111. The London County Council tramway layout was in two distinct halves, north and south. This was partly explained by the existence of separate company systems which were taken over by the L.C.C. In 1905-8, the Kingsway Tramway Subway was built to connect the two halves. Single-deck cars descended the steep gradient shown, ran beneath Kingsway and Aldwych and emerged on Victoria Embankment. A trip-lever system can be seen just above and to the left of the tram; this activated a stop light which remained on until the car reached the first station. There were two intermediate stations reached by stairs from the road. In 1930-31, the subway was deepened to accommodate double-deck trams. Rotary card no. 10497-3, posted from London, 6th February 1914.

112. Well-known locally were Hope Bank Pleasure Grounds at Honley near Huddersfield. Young and old are shown here, captivated by the antics of Punch and Judy. On the right, put to further use many years after its original purpose, can be seen the lower part of a former Huddersfield steam tram trailer body. Lilywhite of Brighouse card no. HNLY.8.

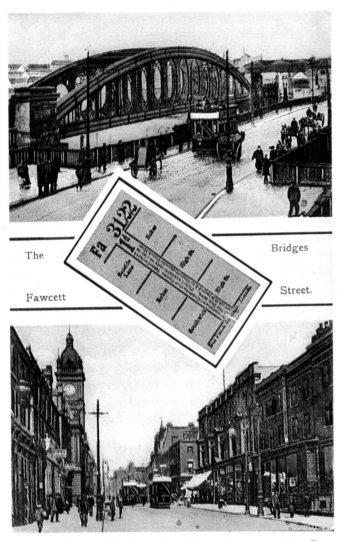

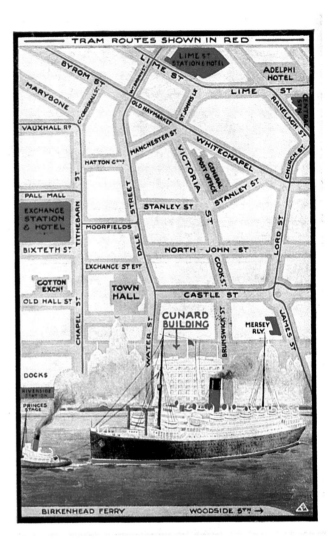

113. The views of Sunderland on this card are not outstanding. The interest lies in the facsimile of a Sunderland Corporation Tramways 1d ticket, printed by the Bell Punch Co., London. Sunderland used roll tickets until 1902 when they were replaced by tickets in racks. These had various values and colours and were known as 'geographical tickets' because of destinations printed on them as shown here. Each route required different tickets. The conductor punched a hole in the destination to which the passenger would travel. Hills of Sunderland 'Aquatint' series card no. S.T.1.

114. This unusual Liverpool postcard, published by the Cunard Company, shows the location of the Cunard Building and, in addition, various city centre railway stations and tram routes.

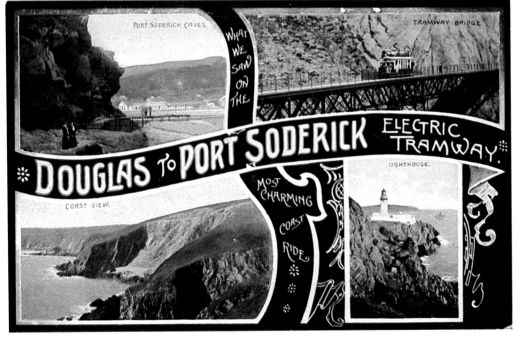

115. This Isle of Man tramway, 4ft. 8½in. gauge and 3¼ miles long, was owned by the Douglas Head Marine Drive Ltd., although it was leased for some years to the Douglas Southern Electric Tramways Ltd. It ran on reserved track along the cliffs and over bridges. With its magnificent scenery, it was a great attraction. There were sixteen open-top double-deck cars with open-sided lower decks; half of these were trailers. The tramway closed in 1939 because of the war and was never re-opened. 'Grosvenor' series card by William Ashton and Sons Ltd., Southport.

DEPOTS

116. The Mexborough and Swinton Tramway Co. operated cars from Rotherham boundary through Rawmarsh and Swinton to the Old Toll Bar at Mexborough. When the system was opened in February 1907, current collection was by Dolter surface contact. In theory, the stud became dead after the car passed over it. In practice, studs frequently remained live. Because of this, in July 1908, the Board of Trade ordered operation to cease and for some weeks, during conversion to overhead power supply, there was no tram service. This depot shot was taken prior to the original opening of the tramway. In the front line, two cars were already on their trucks. Three cars had been lifted on to barrels in readiness for fitting the trucks.

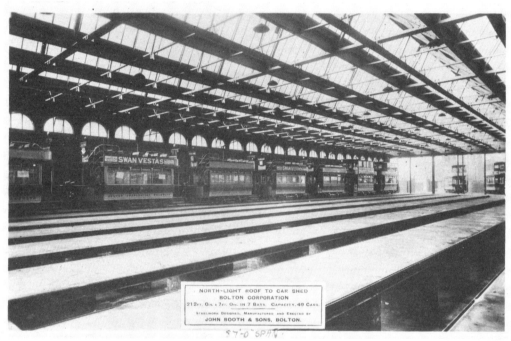

117. This depot was built for Bolton Corporation, whose thirty miles of tram routes radiated from the town centre. The caption informs us that the building had capacity for 49 cars in seven bays and that the steelwork was designed, manufactured and erected by John Booth and Sons of Bolton. Thus, the card was an advert for a local firm.

118. This card shows Blundell Street Depot, Blackpool, closed in 1982 and since demolished. The tram, no. 32, was new in 1901 and originally had an open-top. The days when Blackpool Corporation trams ran inland as well as along the coast are recalled by the nameboard *'Talbot Square, Marton, Central Station'*.

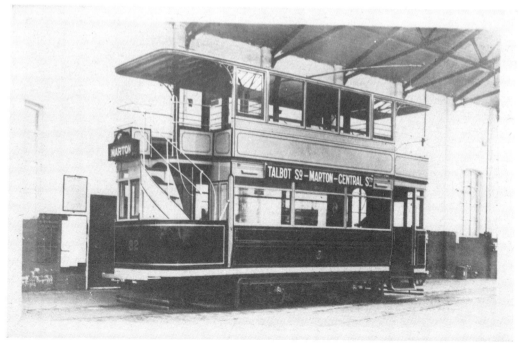

119. These tram maintenance men were assembled in the depot yard at Chingford Road, Walthamstow, Essex, with a tram as backcloth. All were part of the Walthamstow Urban District Council Light Railways. The Robertson's Marmalade advertisement is prominent but note also the adverts on the insides of the lower-deck windows.

120. The elevated position provided an excellent view of the London County Council tram depot at New Cross. Of particular interest is the traverser in the left foreground which was used to convey cars sideways to the required stabling road. Posted from Peckham, 1st August 1907.

121. Although not captioned, the tram destination 'Southwark Bridge' and conduit track signified that this was a London view. It turned out to be the exterior of New Cross Depot shown on the previous card. Postmarked Camberwell, 9th April 1907.

COMIC
CARDS

122. This 'Last Car' type card (artist F. Macleod) could have been overprinted with a town name but has escaped the treatment. Card by H. Garner, Leicester (Living Picture Co.).

For Ease & Rapid Travelling come to Morecambe.

123. Derogatory sayings abound on this scathingly sardonic card. In this case, the overprint is for Morecambe, which had horse trams until 1926. Lawson's series card, Lancaster.

124. The humour is milder on this York card. The city kept its horse trams until 1909. The postcard, published by Delittle, Fenwick and Co., York, was not, as far as is known, used for any other town or city.

THE HILLY BIT OF OLD YORK.

THE POLICEMAN SAID "FOLLOW THE TRAM-LINES."

Where shall I get the tram?
In your back if you don't move,
Ma'am!

125. A card by popular artist Dudley Buxton, published by A.V.N. Jones and Co., Fore Street, London, and posted from that city.

126. Reg Carter, another well-known artist, designed this postcard, published by E. Mack, King Henry's Road, Hampstead, London.

127. Slightly risque by Edwardian standards, this postcard was no. 40 in the 'Forward' series published by John H. King, Birmingham.

128. The inevitable 'Bamforth' and the irresistible fat woman/thin man. Card by Bamforth and Co. Ltd., Holmfirth, series no. 47, postally used on 12th July 1918.

TIMID YOUNG THING—"SHALL I HAVE A SHOCK IF I TREAD ON THE LINE?"
NAUGHTY CONDUCTOR—"NO MISS, NOT UNLESS YOU TOUCH THE OVERHEAD WIRE WITH YOUR OTHER FOOT, THEN WE SHOULD BOTH HAVE A SHOCK!!!"

COPYRIGHT   No. 40   FORWARD SERIES.

GRUMPY LITTLE MAN: "They ought to charge fares by weight on these cars. Some of you would have to pay double then!"
STOUT PARTY: "Well, if that was so, it wouldn't pay them to stop the car to pick up the likes of you!"

Sketched at Wimbledon.

Mrs JOB : Look 'ere, when's that 'ampton court car comin' the bloomin' kids is gettin' 'ungry !!

129. This cartoon card was part of a series of six published by Hutchinson and Co., Wimbledon, and all with a tram theme. Note the perceptive detail and the artist's signature with date.

RIDING ON A TRAM CAR.

Oh, come with me for a ride on top of a tram car,
Into the sweet country air we can go gliding far,
As the car hums along no other can hear
The sweet words of love we can whisper up there,
I can squeeze you so tightly; there's nothing to fear,
When riding on a tram car.

420

130. The top of a tramcar may not have been the ideal location to perpetrate romantic inclinations but the theme provided an excuse for this song type card, no. 420 in the 'Living Picture' Series of Henry Garner of Leicester.

131. This card, published by W.V. Cole of Exeter, is not an overprint type. When compared with photographic illustration no. 8, it will be observed that the drawing shows an actual Exeter horse tram, albeit with addition of spider's web and predatory looking bird. Posted from Exeter.

A bit of Old Exeter.

UNUSUAL

132. Earlier reference has been made to tramways in Morecambe. After Morecambe Corporation purchased the section from East View to Battery Inn in 1908, the Battery Inn to Strawberry Gardens section, which still belonged to the Morecambe Tramways Co., was converted to an unusual internal combustion system. Four single-deck trams with Leyland petrol engines ran until 1926. One is shown here at the start of operations.

133. In 1915, a batch of 150 trailer cars were built by Brush for the London County Council fleet. They were used on certain services in South London until 1924. The fleet numbers had a 'T' prefix. In this view can be seen the coupling for attaching to the towing tram and the gates which were fitted across the space between tram and trailer to prevent people walking through.

134. The Great Orme Tramways Co. opened a cable tramway from Llandudno up Great Orme in 1902 (lower section) and 1903 (upper section). It was municipalised in 1948 and still operates during the holiday season with four of the original seven cars. (The other three were trailer cars which went out of use following an accident due to coupling failure). The system is in two separate halves with two cars on each. On the lower half, the cable is in a conduit, visible in this view; on the upper half, the cable is exposed. The trolley arm shown has nothing to do with current collection; it is part of the signalling system which enables the driver to telephone the winding-engine man. H.H.H. Photo Art series card.

Tram Car, Portstewart.

135. A short 3ft. gauge roadside steam tramway linked the village of Portstewart on the north coast of Ireland with the nearest station on the mainline railway. Opened in 1882, it was purchased by the Belfast and Northern Counties Railway Co. in 1897 and operated until 1926. There were three steam tram engines (built by Kitson and Co. Ltd., Leeds), one single-deck toastrack, two double-deck tramcars and one van (examples of the two latter are shown here). Dickson's 'Ulster' series card.

136. Even in Edwardian times, there would have been an element of surprise on seeing this combination for the first time. Linking Wolverton and Stony Stratford, Buckinghamshire, this 3ft. 6in. gauge roadside steam tramway was opened in 1887. It was taken over by the London and North Western Railway Co. in 1920 and survived until 1926, never being electrified. The car pictured was one of three which were 44 feet long and seated over a hundred people. Another car seated eighty, whilst the fifth had seats for only fifty. During the tramway's lifetime, there were seven engines. Card by Alfred E. Tyrrell, Abington Street, Northampton.

WOLVERTON & STONY, STRATFORD.
TRAM CAR & ENGINE.

TRAMMING TIN STONE, EAST POOL MINE, NEAR REDRUTH.

137. In addition to carrying passengers, a few tramways had industrial uses. One example was the Camborne and Redruth Tramways which had a contract to carry tin-ore from East Poole Mine to the smelting works. For this purpose, two electric locomotives (no. 2 is shown) and fourteen side-tipping mineral wagons were used. Card by E.S., London, no. 3005.

SINGLE-DECK TRAMS

138. Twenty of these cars, built by Brush, were acquired by the Metropolitan Electric Tramways Ltd. in 1905 for the Alexandra Palace routes, where steep gradients required the use of track brakes. On the Alexandra Palace East route, a low railway bridge in Station Road also restricted the trams to single-deckers. Originally, these cars had a non-smoking compartment, just visible on the right of this view. The partitions were soon removed; presumably smoking was then prohibited completely.

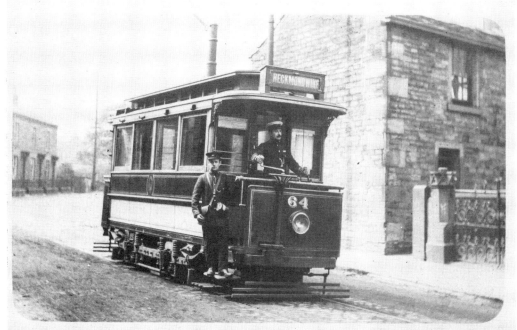

139. Six of these small twenty-seater cars were built by the Brush Electrical Engineering Co. Ltd., Loughborough, in 1904 for the Yorkshire (Woollen District) Electric Tramways Ltd. They were used mainly in the Cleckheaton/Heckmondwike area. After five of the cars had been offered for sale without success in 1923, it was decided to convert four of them into two longer trams. This produced two seven-window cars, with seating capacity for 36, which were used chiefly on the Dewsbury/Ravensthorpe route.

140. The inhabitants of the valley, which stretched northwards from Waterfoot to Water, would be pleased when a tram service was introduced by Rawtenstall Corporation from 21st January 1911. Stone-built houses provided a background to this all-enclosed car, built by the United Electric Car Co. Ltd., Preston. The card was posted from Lumb, one of the places on the route, on 12th July 1911.

OPEN-TOP TRAMS

141. This tram, built in 1900 at the Electric Railway and Tramway Carriage Works Ltd., Preston, was photographed at Whitley Bay. It belonged to the Tynemouth and District Electric Traction Co. Ltd. (another B.E.T. subsidiary company) whose gauge was 3ft. 6in. Part of a long message on the back reads *'The chap that's on this car has just got his notice for lying idle. What do you think of that. Champion. I have never stopped washing dishes and cleaning spoons etc. this week. Mary wants a chap again. There is a young lady stopping here from Ferryhill. She had a bath this morning and nearly swallowed all the water'.* Postmarked at Whitley Bay.

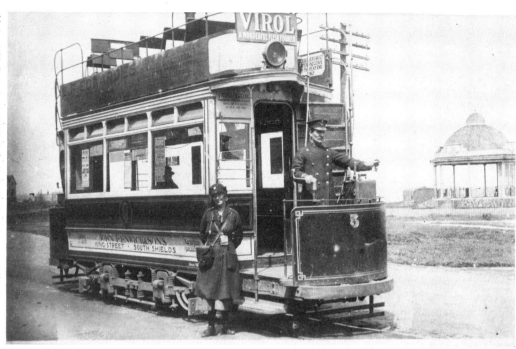

142. Halifax Corporation was reputed to have the hilliest tramway trystem in the country. Eleven routes were operated, the longest being along the Calder Valley to Hebden Bridge. Halifax never had horse or steam trams; electric routes were opened from 1898 onwards. The gauge was 3ft. 6in., thus precluding through running with the nearby towns of Bradford, Dewsbury and Huddersfield who had different gauges. A ride on the upper deck of this tram would have been a summer rather than a winter pursuit. Rain, snow or shine, the driver had no choice. Card posted at Halifax in August 1908.

143. Barrow-in-Furness, Lancashire, had an isolated tramway system which was worked directly by the British Electric Traction Co. Ltd. (many tramways were B.E.T. owned but usually operated through a subsidiary company). The card shows car no. 2, built by Brush in 1903, and probably in new condition because it carried no adverts. The tramways were acquired by the Corporation on 1st January 1920. Card by W. Cookson.

144. At Laneshawbridge, in Lancashire Pennine country, but near the Yorkshire border, is shown car no. 9 of the Colne and Trawden Light Railways Co. It was one of four built by Brush in 1905. (A light railway was authorised by Light Railway Order under the Light Railways Act of 1896 whereas a tramway was laid by authority of the Tramways Act of 1870. This explains why some systems, which had all the characteristics of a tramway, were called light railways). This system was taken over by Colne Corporation in 1914 and by Burnley, Colne and Nelson Joint Transport Committee in 1933. It closed in 1934. Photo by J. Wilkinson, Colne.

145. Chesterfield Corporation worked a 4ft. 8½in. gauge route from Brampton through Chesterfield to Whittington Moor, total length 3⅝ miles. Tram no. 7 is shown in Chatsworth Road on the Brampton section during trials which began in early December 1904. The tramway was opened on 23rd December; this card by C.H. Nadin, a local photographer, was posted from Chesterfield on 24th December 1904. The message made no reference to the trams, but was a 'thank-you' for Christmas presents.

146. Exeter Corporation operated a 3ft. 6in. gauge electric tramway from 1905 to 1931, following acquisition of the horse system of the Exeter Tramways Co. Ltd. in 1903. Car no. 11, shown outside St. David's Station, was part of the first batch of trams and was built at the Electric Railway and Tramway Carriage Works Ltd., Preston. They were numbered 1 to 12, 14 and 15, but not no. 13, presumably on grounds of superstition.

147. Torquay had no trams of any kind until 1907 when the Torquay Tramways Co. Ltd. opened its first routes, with a gauge of 3ft. 6in. Extensions were made in subsequent years, the last being to Paignton in 1911. Originally operated on the Dolter stud surface contact system, the Paignton extension used overhead wire and other routes were then changed to this. During summer months, special tourist cars were operated on the circular route through Babbacombe. One is shown here; this must be a pre-1911 view because the car has no overhead equipment. Photo by Pyne, Croft Road, Torre, Torquay.

148. The only tramway in Cornwall was of 3ft. 6in. gauge and linked the tin-mining towns of Camborne and Redruth, approximately three miles apart. Car no. 1, shown at West End, Redruth, had inaugurated the system in 1902. There were five other similar cars and two single-deckers. The passenger system closed in 1927 although the mineral traffic, mentioned earlier, survived until 1934.

149. Leicester Corporation worked electric trams from 1904 until closure in 1949. Operation began with 99 cars of the type shown here, built by the Electric Railway and Tramway Carriage Works Ltd., Preston. 1905 deliveries consisted of double-deckers with both open and covered tops. Subsequently all open-top trams were fitted with top covers; eventually many were rebuilt as totally enclosed cars. This card was postally used from Leicester on 26th July 1915. The army recruitment posters in the lower-deck windows suggest the photograph was taken during the war. Note the grill behind the conductor which was closed or opened depending on which way the tram was going (people normally boarded/alighted at the rear). The stairway, known as reversed type, would prevent the driver from seeing properly to his left, hence the perforations, visible only on the rear stair.

150. In 1903, the Metropolitan Electric Tramways Ltd. placed an order with Brush of Loughborough for the supply of 150 trams (with spare parts) at a cost of £119,360. Seventy were of the type seen here, sixty as on illustration 107 and twenty as illustration 138. Tram no. 31 was delivered in 1904; the card is postmarked Tottenham, 8th March 1905, so the car is probably shown in original condition. It differed from the Leicester tram by having eight wheels, unusual spaced windows, scrollwork around the upper-deck and a direct type of staircase which gave better vision to the driver.

TRANSITION

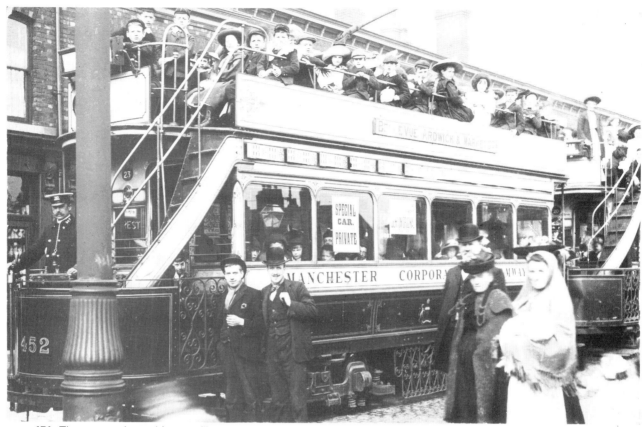

151. The two cards on this page illustrate the alterations which could be made to a tramcar. In 1902-3, Manchester Corporation took delivery from Brush, Loughborough, of fifty bogie cars, numbered 437 to 486. Tram no. 452 is illustrated here, probably in as-delivered condition. It was on private hire, filled with children, possibly on a trip to Belle Vue pleasure grounds. Four cars in this batch had top covers added about 1904.

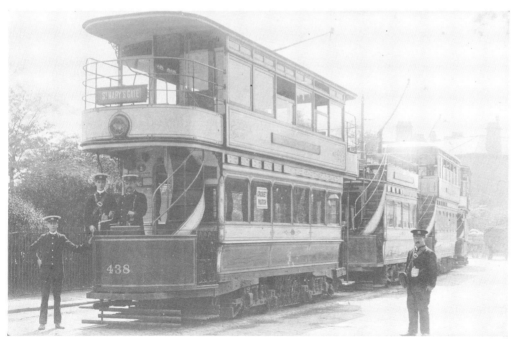

152. Between 1907 and 1916, remaining trams in the 437 to 486 batch were given a rather more modern appearance by having top covers fitted, plus end balconies added and stairways modified, as shown here on car no. 438. Despite these changes, the original part of the tram can easily be detected. Behind 438 are a smaller four-wheel car, a balloon bogie car, so called because of the slightly domed roof, and a similar car to 438.

COVERED TRAMS

153. As would be expected, this Preston Corporation tram was built at the Electric Railway and Tramway Carriage Works in Preston. When new in 1904, it had an open upper-deck; the top cover was added about 1908 but contributed little towards giving the tram a more modern appearance. Although the gauge was 4ft. 8½in., the car had a lank look, accentuated by the tall narrow upper-deck windows. Passengers would ride in some comfort inside and, for a fine day, there were seats on the small balconies. But the driver had little protection from the elements. Preston's trams covered 10½ miles of route and were withdrawn between 1932 and 1935.

154. Stockport Corporation operated electric trams from 1901 until they were replaced by motor-buses in 1949-51. The tram illustrated was part of a batch delivered in 1906-7 from the United Electric Car Co. Ltd., Preston (formerly Electric Railway and Tramway Carriage Works Ltd.). The card was postmarked Stockport, 12th February 1910. The message reads *'Just a card hoping you are all well. This is one of the Stockport cars. I daresay you recognise the guard and the other is his driver'*.

155. The London County Council eventually had 123 miles of track operated on the conduit principle and 27 miles operated from overhead wires. At 21 places there were changeover points where trams were changed from one system to the other. The large bogie car shown, no. 978, was part of the famous E1 batch introduced from 1907 onwards and was working from overhead wiring. The view must date from 1912, the year of the Latin-British Exhibition at White City, which was advertised below the upper deck windows.

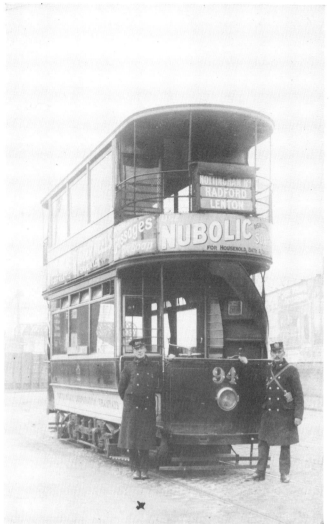

156. This Nottingham Corporation tram had been built in 1902 with an open upper-deck. Visible on the original card, through a magnifier, is the word 'Motorman' on the driver's cap. On many tramway systems, drivers were known as motormen and conductors as guards. The extensive Nottingham system was abandoned during 1927-36, mostly in favour of trolleybuses. Note the ink cross beneath the motorman. Although the back of the card (not postally used) does not have a repeat of the cross, there is a handwritten note *'Died 27th March 1931, aged 55.'*

157. With its destination 'Kirkstall Abbey', advert for *'The Yorkshire Post'* and exceptionally large fleet number, this tram is easily recognisable as belonging to Leeds Corporation. It was part of a batch built at the Kirkstall Road Works of Leeds City Tramways between 1913 and 1915. The back of the card, not postally used, has the brief message *'May 1st 1923, love, Harry'.* This suggests the tram was approximately nine years old when photographed (one of the same batch was in service until 1948). It is shown in as-built condition with enclosed vestibules (for driver protection) and open balconies (the delight of small boys).

158. This unique bogie car, no. 572, belonged to Liverpool Corporation. Built in 1912 by the United Electric Car Co. Ltd., it had the unusual central entrance/exit and seated 83 people but gave little protection to the driver. Not being an unqualified success, no more were constructed and this prototype was withdrawn after a few years.

TOASTRACKS

PWLLHELI. N.W.

159. The resort of Pwllheli in North Wales had two separate 3ft. 6in. gauge horse tramways. The Pwllheli and Llanbedrog Tramway ran along the coast between the two places in its title. It originated as a quarry line and closed in 1928 after the sea had claimed a section of track. Pwllheli Urban District Council operated the other tramway between the railway station and beach. It closed in 1920. This card shows one of the Pwllheli and Llanbedrog toastrack cars in Cardiff Road, probably a few years before closure. F.H. May handprinted real photo view.

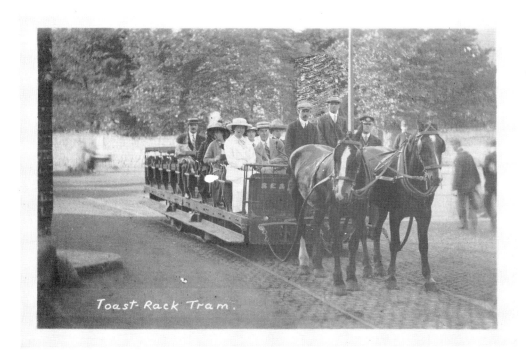

Toast-Rack Tram.

160. The Folkestone, Sandgate and Hythe Tramway Co. operated a 4ft. 8½in. gauge horse tramway from 1884 which, despite the title, only ran between Sandgate and Hythe. Taken over by the South-Eastern Railway (later South-Eastern and Chatham Railway) in 1893, it was never electrified and was abandoned in 1921. The card shows that two horses were required to pull this toastrack which was larger than the one in the previous view. Posted from Hythe, 5th August 1920.

161. Ideal for a tour at the seaside on a sunny day were the electric toastracks. This was one of seven which belonged to Southport Corporation and initially offered a seven mile trip around the town for 6d (children 3d). Similar cars were used at Blackpool, Llandudno and Portsmouth. Southport Corporation also had conventional trams. Some routes were operated by a separate concern, the Southport Tramways Co. Ltd. Postally used from Southport on 5th July 1915.

WORK

162. Tramcars, particularly the larger examples, excelled at moving crowds of people. This card, according to the caption, shows workmen's cars outside the Carron Iron Works at Falkirk. The trams were well loaded with workers. Children were in attendance, probably eager to be photographed. The cars belonged to the Falkirk and District Tramways Co. who operated a 4ft. gauge circular route, plus one branch, from 1905 to 1936. Card no. 521 in the F.B. series.

163. Oldham Corporation operated ten routes to 4ft. 8½in. gauge which were opened between 1900 and 1905 (an extension from Moorside to Grains Bar was opened in 1914) and abandoned between 1935 and 1939. They did, however, continue to operate, jointly with Manchester Corporation, the service from Waterhead through Oldham to Manchester until closure on 3rd August 1946. Oldham Corporation tram no. 13 is shown loading with workmen. Built in 1901 as a single-deck bogie car, it seated 36 people. In 1903, it was given an enclosed upper-deck, the staircases were placed inside the car body and the seating was increased to 78. No other trams in the batch were so treated.

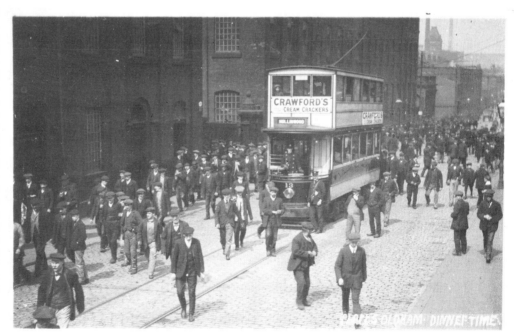

PLEASURE

After the Fair, Portsdown Hill

164. These Portsmouth Corporation trams were caught busily loading passengers after a day out. Car no. 70 in the foreground would, according to its destination indicator, travel via Fratton Bridge to South Parade Pier, Southsea, four miles away. Printed card no. 362 published by A. Eden Smith, Cosham.

165. Most of the people shown here were attired in their best clothes and had clustered upstairs on these early Aberdeen trams to ensure inclusion in the photograph. The Aberdeen District Tramways Co. operated horse lines from 1874. These were taken over by Aberdeen Corporation in 1898, electrified from 1899 to 1902 and new routes subsequently opened. Despite modernisation, with streamlined trams introduced as late as 1949 and depot enlargements made in 1951, the final trams ran in 1958.

166. The National United Order of Free Gardeners was a Friendly Society (which provided sick benefits etcetera) whose Olive Lodge was situated at the Reindeer Inn, Cleveland Street, in the Groves area of Hull. On 18th August 1906, they took all children whose parents were insured with the Society on a tram tour of Hull, advertising the Society, particularly in the richer areas, as they went. Here, the tour had paused in Spring Bank on the way to Pearson Park. These and many other Hull trams started life with open upper-decks, top covers being fitted between 1903 and 1909. Electric trams ran in Hull from 1899 to 1945, many of the routes being switched to trolleybuses. Postally used from Hull, 4th September 1906.

TERMINI

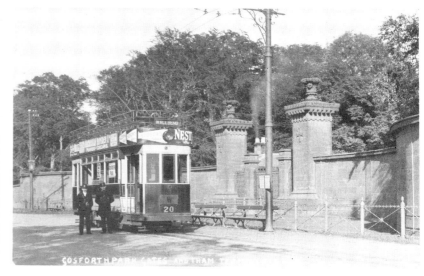

167. Trams of both Newcastle Corporation and the Tyneside Tramways and Tramroads Co. could be seen outside Gosforth Park. This view shows car no. 20 of the Tramroads Company awaiting passengers before beginning the 36-minute run to Wallsend. At the side of the car are seats for the weary and on the pole a time-table display. Constructed in 1904 by Brush of Loughborough, the tram had tongued and grooved panelling around the vestibule ends, which gave a pleasing appearance.

168. This bogie car, photographed in front of the village green at Norton, near Stockton-on-Tees, was built by G.F. Milnes and Co. Ltd., Birkenhead, in 1898. It belonged to the Imperial Tramways Co. Ltd., who operated 3ft. 6in. gauge lines in the Middlesbrough/Stockton area. Unlike other tramways, the gauge here was measured between groove centres so, compared with other lines, was actually 3ft. 7in. In 1921, the system was divided into three parts which went to Middlesbrough, Stockton and Thornaby Corporations. The Stockton and Thornaby portions were operated through a Joint Committee. The tram shown here was re-allocated to Middlesbrough.

169. Horse, steam and electric trams; trolleybuses and motorbuses. All have operated in hilly Bradford at some time. Gradually, from 1898 onwards, Bradford Corporation introduced electric trams, with a track gauge of 4ft. Here, car no. 7 of the first batch of sixteen, built in 1898, was photographed at Eccleshill terminus to the north-east of the city. Its destination: the well-known Forster Square in the centre of Bradford. On the left are interesting shops, including the post-office, and beyond them the Mechanic's Institute.

170. This tram, at New Ferry terminus, Birkenhead, had an unusual appearance, which can be explained as follows. The batch, built in 1900, started life as bogie single-deckers with clerestory roofs and were confined to the New Ferry route which had a low bridge. In the hope of providing a satisfactory service with fewer cars, they were rebuilt in 1908/9 as low-height flat-roofed double-deckers with centre knifeboard seating upstairs. The lower deck gangway headroom was provided beneath this knifeboard seating. Thus, the low bridge was negotiated and the same number of passengers was carried with a less frequent service. Everyone was happy, except perhaps the passengers. Other Birkenhead Corporation trams were of more conventional design.

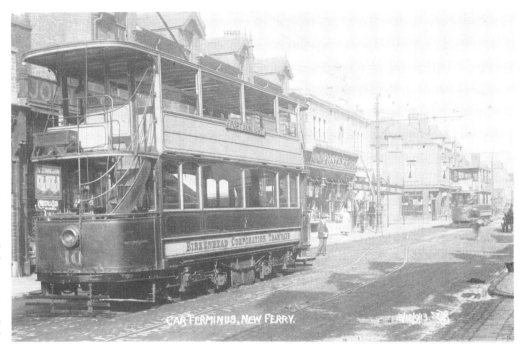

171. Sheffield Corporation had a large progressive tramway system. Steel metropolis maybe, but this is not evident in the view of Fulwood terminus to the west of the city, near the edge of the Derbyshire Peak District. Tram no. 149, delivered as an open-topper in 1901, later had a short top cover fitted, as seen here. The photographer caught the conductor swivelling the trolley-arm with a bamboo pole for the return journey. This was a necessary ritual at most termini before the introduction of trolley reversers. Valentine's X.L. series card no. 64412 JV.

172. Car no. 10 of the Ilford Council Tramways was caught at Chadwell Heath, Essex, before starting its journey to Barking. Built by Hurst Nelson and Co. Ltd. of Motherwell, it was delivered in 1903. Eventually, top covers were purchased and fitted to this and other similar trams. As can be seen, the lower-deck Tudor-arch style windows were repeated on the top-deck to provide some harmony, but the cover still looks slightly incongruous. Posted from Chadwell Heath, 19th October 1921.

173. Tram no. 151 of the Metropolitan Electric Tramways Ltd. is seen at Stonebridge terminus. Built by Brush in 1906, it received a top cover about 1914 and became part of the London Passenger Transport Board fleet in 1933. In 1936, the whole of the western side of the former M.E.T. system, which included Stonebridge, was converted to trolleybus operation. Robinson series card.

174. With road and verges in unkempt condition, tram no. 11 of Maidstone Corporation had arrived at Loose terminus. The Corporation only had 5½ miles of 3ft. 6in. gauge track, worked by seventeen cars similar to that shown, plus a single-deck demi-car for one-man operation. This tramway was abandoned in 1928-30, trolleybuses being substituted on some routes. Card postmarked Boughton Monchelsea (this was a few miles south of Loose), 16th March 1909.

TRAM TERMINUS, LOOSE.

175. At Rainham, typical Kentish buildings and delightful animation provided additional interest to this tram scene. The car belonged to the Chatham and District Light Railway Co. whose 3ft. 6in. gauge system included reserved track to Rainham. Card from Eastgate series, published by W. Nayler, 212 High Street, Rochester, posted from Rainham.

MODERNISATION

VICAR LANE AND MARKET BUILDINGS. LEEDS

GBL/64

CHADWICK STUDIO PRODUCTIONS

176. This view epitomises Leeds trams in the nineteen-fifties, a struggle between old and new. The middle-distance tram was part of a large batch built in 1930-32 and called Horsfields after the transport manager. Although of dated appearance when introduced, they had modern equipment and performed superbly. Nearer the camera, with some concessions to modernisation, no. 513 was one of the large batch of London Feltham trams, built in 1930-31 and purchased from London Transport in 1950. (The name originated from their construction at the Union Construction Co. works at Feltham, Middlesex). Not shown, but worth a mention in relation to modernisation, are the two continental-style single-deck railcars which proved unpopular, also the miles of reserved sleeper track on the city outskirts. The decision in 1953 to scrap the trams might have been reversed because of opposing local political opinions. The last trams ran in 1959. Card no. GBL/64 of Chadwick Studio Productions, 491 Oakwood Lane, Leeds.

HORSE TRAMCAR 1894

OPEN TOP TRAMCAR 1903

STANDARD OPEN FRONT TRAMCAR 1914

CORONATION TRAMCAR 1938.

THE CITY OF GLASGOW

TRAMCARS
THE FIRST TO THE LAST.
1894 TO 1ST. SEPT. 1962.

177. This card was issued in 1962 to commemorate the end of Glasgow Corporation Tramways. It provides a précis of Glasgow trams and, apart from the omission of steam, of trams in general. In its heyday, the Glasgow system was second only to London in size. The 'Coronation' tramcars (bottom right) which were introduced from 1937 onwards were Glasgow's attempt at modernisation, some being built as late as 1954. Running alongside the 'Coronations' were an abundance of old cars. The cost of replacing these with modern trams was estimated to be more than for replacement with buses and trolleybuses. And so Glasgow lost its trams. Millar and Lang National series card.

178. In 1985, Blackpool celebrated its tramway centenary. It was also the centenary of electric street tramways in the British Isles. In the nineteen-thirties, Blackpool Corporation embarked on a great tramway modernisation programme. The four types of streamlined tram which were introduced are shown here. In design, they were ahead of their time. Fifty years later, many of these cars are still operating, albeit with some alteration. Card no. G 4567 by Valentines of Dundee.

179. Several postcards of the new trams were issued. This prototype luxury railcoach was delivered in early 1934 and placed on display. Favourable comments were received; subsequently eleven more were ordered and delivered (with slightly higher sides) in time for the summer season. They replaced the toastracks and became known as open boat cars. Several are still in use when weather permits. Note that this photograph was included in the multi-view card above with the chimney 'demolished'. Card published by M. Miller and Co., Blackpool.

180. This card, from the 'thirties, shows each of the four types of new streamlined tram, plus an old toastrack and a Lytham St. Annes Corporation double-decker. Five decades later, the scene is not vastly different. Trams continue to stop here, near North Pier and opposite Talbot Square. Long may it be so. SS Photos, card no. E 4854.